ideals®
MOTHER'S DAY

*I wish you
all the joy a heart can hold,
with faith to lead the way;
wishes come true, a hundred-fold;
and a happy Mother's Day.*

—IRENE LARSEN

IDEALS PUBLICATIONS

NASHVILLE, TENNESSEE

A Mother's Love

Emily Taylor

There is not a grand, inspiring thought,
there is not a truth by wisdom taught,
there is not a feeling pure and high
that may not be read in a mother's eye.

There are teachings in earth and sky and air—
the heavens the glory of God declare—
but louder than voice, beneath, above,
He is heard to speak through a mother's love.

The Mothers of the Earth

Grace Noll Crowell

The woman who has borne a child,
we pause to honor her today;
the woman who has led a child
with patience down life's broad highway;
the woman who has God's own heart,
His tenderness and gentle grace,
who comes to Him for needed strength,
who meets Him daily face to face.

The woman who a thousand times
would bear her agony of pain
to save her child from needless hurt;
to keep him clean and free from stain;

to know that he would walk at last
a man across the world's bright sod,
an honor to his land, his flag;
a glory to his home, his God.

The woman who has borne a child—
no one may choose a better part.
The woman who is kind and wise,
who moves with quiet mind and heart,
whose love surrounds a little child
to meet his daily, constant need,
who spends her life that he may live—
we honor her today indeed.

The Hand That Rocks the Cradle

William Ross Wallace

Blessings on the hand of women!
Angels guard its strength and grace.
In the palace, cottage, hovel,
oh, no matter where the place;
would that never storms assailed it,
rainbows ever gently curled,
for the hand that rocks the cradle
is the hand that rules the world.

Infancy's the tender fountain,
power may with beauty flow,
mothers first to guide the streamlets,
from them souls unresting grow—
grow on for the good or evil,
sunshine streamed or evil hurled,
for the hand that rocks the cradle
is the hand that rules the world.

Woman, how divine your mission,
here upon our natal sod;
keep—oh, keep the young heart open
always to the breath of God!
All true trophies of the ages
are from mother-love impearled,
for the hand that rocks the cradle
is the hand that rules the world.

Blessings on the hand of women!
Fathers, sons, and daughters cry,
and the sacred song is mingled
with the worship in the sky—
mingles where no tempest darkens,
rainbows evermore are hurled;
for the hand that rocks the cradle
is the hand that rules the world.

100 YEARS
OF MOTHER'S DAY IN AMERICA

One hundred years ago, Mother's Day was officially established in the United States, when President Woodrow Wilson issued a presidential proclamation that declared the second Sunday of May a holiday. The day we now celebrate with greeting cards, breakfasts in bed, and carnations in church had its origins in women's groups who promoted peace and unity, particularly during and after the Civil War. These efforts were led by women such as Julia Ward Howe and Ann Reeves Jarvis, whose daughter is widely credited for creating the Mother's Day we know today. In 1907, as a way of continuing the work of her mother, Anna Jarvis began a national letter-writing campaign asking members of Congress and all Americans to set aside a special day honoring mothers. A devoted daughter, Miss Jarvis had lost her mother a few years earlier, and she hoped to persuade others to recognize the importance of mothers' love and dedication. A year later, at Jarvis's request, her church in Philadelphia, Pennsylvania, celebrated the first Mother's Day. The idea spread rapidly throughout the country. By 1914, celebrating Mother's Day had become so popular that Congress declared the day a national holiday and President Woodrow Wilson called for a nationwide celebration. The holiday was quickly embraced by the American people and the custom of a designated day to celebrate mothers was solidified.

CONGRESSIONAL RESOLUTION, 1914

Whereas the service rendered the United States by the American mother is the greatest source of the country's strength and admiration; and Whereas we honor ourselves and the mothers of America when we do any thing to give emphasis to the home as the fountainhead of the State; and Whereas the American mother is doing so much for good government and humanity, we declare that the second Sunday of May will henceforth be celebrated as Mother's Day.

PRESIDENTIAL PROCLAMATION, MAY 9, 1914

I, Woodrow Wilson, President of the United States of America, . . . do invite the people of the United States to display the flag at their homes or other suitable places on the second Sunday in May as a public expression of our love and reverence for the mothers of our country. —*President Woodrow Wilson*

Painting by George Hinke. Image © Ideals Publications

Home

Mary Loberg

Home to me is laughter,
kisses on the cheek,
warm looks and tender touches
when the heart's too full to speak.
Home is sharing happiness
and dreams I'm dreaming of—
home to me is Mother,
home to me is love.

Mother's Day

Elisabeth Weaver Winstead

Mother's love is a precious thing
that deepens through the years,
in memory of bright sunshine days,
of laughter, love, and tears.

Mother's love is a treasured thing;
though far afield we roam,
the cherished bonds of faith and love
still pull our hearts toward home.

Photograph © Elena Elisseeva/Shutterstock

MOTHER'S DAY CARDS

Marie B. Fouts

As I go about my work in a card shop, I look at the racks of Mother's Day cards. Beautiful cards, verses and all dedicated to Mother, some written in calligraphy, others in script or in bold print; there are so many choices, one could find any type of card for any mother. As I walk along the racks, my mind wanders back to the cards I received from my son and daughter.

I think the first ones I received might have been made in Sunday school. The teachers had my children copy words on a card they made, often on construction paper with their precious little handprints drawn on the paper and a poem about small handprints on the wall, wishing me a happy Mother's Day—so eagerly presented to me as soon as I arrived to pick them up at the classroom door.

Later, they made them in school where the teachers would have them create their own verses. The cards usually told me they loved me and to have a happy Mother's Day. My son's were always very short, since he did not like to write, but my daughter's were long and rhyming, often following the same pattern as her brother's. One such Mother's Day card from her read:

> To a mom I dearly love, she was brought to me from above.
> I love her like I do no other, a whole lot more than my brother!

I smiled as I read the poem. The sentiment was so sweet. I was so glad to be loved more than her brother, but he wasn't! My son's poem read: "A mother is caring and not made for sharing!" My son had decorated his card with many hearts and flowers, since he loved to draw.

I saved most of these cards and look at them from time to time. My son is no longer with us, but my daughter, now with a family of her own, thoughtfully chooses sentiments properly written on bond paper from the accomplished poet, usually from the card shop where I work.

But I still cherish the broadly traced script, painstakingly written with the handprints on construction paper. These are the cards I treasure the most.

As I walk down the rows of Mother's Day cards, I know none can compare. Those handmade, handwritten cards let you know you are truly loved. They are written by the children who live with you day in and day out. They know your shortcomings and your love and take time to make you a special Mother's Day card, and in them, you find your affirmation as a mother!

Bits & Pieces

*Her children
call her blessed.*
—Proverbs 31:28

And so our mothers and grandmothers have, more often
than not, anonymously handed on the creative spark, the
seed of the flower they themselves never hoped to see—
or like a sealed letter they could not plainly read.
—Alice Walker

I drank in, as a plant from the soil, the first nourishing juices
of my young intellect from the books carefully selected by my
mother. But I drank deep, above all, from my mother's mind.
—Alphonse de Lamartine

For when you looked into my mother's eyes
you knew, as if He had told you, why God sent
her into the world—it was to open the minds
of all who looked, to beautiful thoughts.
—J. M. Barrie

My mother had a great
deal of trouble with me,
but I think she enjoyed it.
—*Mark Twain*

My mother is a poem
I'll never be able to write,
though everything I write
is a poem to my mother.
—*Sharon Doubiago*

When I stopped seeing
my mother with the
eyes of a child, I saw the
woman who helped me
give birth to myself.
—*Nancy Friday*

Into a woman's keeping is
committed the destiny of the
generations to come after us.
—*Theodore Roosevelt*

Who ran to help me when I fell
and would some pretty story tell
or kiss the place to make it well?
My mother.
—*Ann Taylor*

A mother's arms are made of tenderness
and children sleep soundly in them.
—*Victor Hugo*

The mother's image is the first that
stamps itself on the unwritten page
of the young child's mind.
—*David O. McKay*

Mother's love is peace.
It need not be acquired; it
need not be deserved.
—*Erich Fromm*

THANK YOU, MOM!

Bea Bourgeois

As part of their handmade Mother's Day gifts last year, the children in my youngest son's fifth grade class wrote personal letters to their moms. Along with the rest of those grade-school Mother's Day presents, his letter has been carefully tucked away to become part of family folklore.

On lined paper, decorated with colored pens and with a blue ribbon at the top, David declared that "My Mother deserves the 'Mother of the Year Award' because she doesn't mind if I get my pants dirty or my shirt. And another thing is she will play poker with me till midnight. What's so neat is she doesn't mind cleaning fish. Last night we got thirty pounds of smelt and she helped! One more thing I like about my mom is she is not scared of mice, hamsters, or gerbils. My mom also sometimes makes my bed and I like that."

The letter is a treasure, even though it describes my household as a rodent-infested gambling casino, smelling of fish and populated by youngsters in soiled clothing heading wearily toward their unmade beds at midnight. No pompous sentiments; no hearts and flowers; just a straightforward "thank you" that only an honest ten-year-old could write.

Although his brothers are older now, and their gifts are becoming somewhat more sophisticated, my elder sons also brightened that second Sunday in May with homemade trinkets. The cardboard box in the attic holds all kinds of mementos that were drawn, colored, pasted, and stapled by little-boy fingers.

One of my favorites was a cottage cheese carton, tastefully camouflaged in pastel tissue paper with a strip of construction paper for its handle. The "basket" was filled with pink and yellow flowers of unknown paper varieties, less than carefully glued to their cardboard stems. Two dozen long-stemmed roses would not have meant as much—and certainly wouldn't have lasted all these years.

David's reference to rodents was not unfounded. The animals in residence at our house (in cages) now number two gerbils named Gladys and Dolores, one black and white mouse named Cousin Gerald, and a fine, fat hamster named Albert Hendryx. Somehow I inherited the late-night feeding routine, and I report to the boys the next morning on the silly antics the little animals staged in their delight over a handful of sunflower seeds.

So it is not surprising that one son confided to a local shopkeeper, "My mother likes rodents!" as he selected a dear, small china mouse as a Mother's Day gift. This same lad has provided me with my own menagerie of stuffed creatures—squirrels, rabbits, mice—and a little statue that looks something like a Tasmanian devil.

Mink coats may come and yachts may go, but mothers understand what real treasures are: the plaster cast of a small second-grade-sized hand; the wall hanging that says, simply, "Thank You, Mom!" in brilliant colors; the booklet made out of construction paper and bound with a piece of yarn, containing pictures illustrating "What My Mom Does for Me." I love the stick figure stirring a huge pot of spaghetti sauce or bending over to zip a zipper. I haven't been that thin in years.

Baby's Feet

Mary Felton

Only two baby's feet, so pink and fair,
so small I hold them both within my hands,
and bending low I kiss them tenderly
with thoughts which none but mothers understand.
I note each line of dainty baby grace,
which those dear feet unconsciously possess.
Dear dimpled feet, how long or short a way
you have to journey, who can tell or guess?

Dear little feet that lie yet all unstained
by contact with a world by sin defiled—
my mother-heart prays God most fervently
that He will guide those restless feet, my child,
and bending o'er thy peaceful couch, I ask
unanswered questions of the future days;
I long to know if these dear feet will tread
upward or down, through rough or pleasant ways.

I cannot tell; it is not mine to know
what God in wisdom for my child hath planned.
And it is best, dear one, that it is so;
for human reason might not understand.
But He who guides the timid sparrow's flight
when it has fluttered from its sheltered home
will not forget my child by day or night
where'er or far those baby feet may roam.

LILACS

Diane Skinner

But thanks be to God, who in Christ always leads us in triumph,
and through us spreads the fragrance of the knowledge of him everywhere.
—2 CORINTHIANS 2:14 (RSV)

"Here, Mommy," exploded five-year-old Heather as she dumped lilac pickings into my hand.

As I readied a milk-glass pitcher to serve as my vase, I headily breathed in their fragrance. Soon a sweet, spicy odor flooded the room.

While the children scampered about the kitchen getting a beater and bowls for cookie dough, I was keenly aware of the pungent smell and its spreading effects. Only a few small blossoms had filled up the room.

What was it the scripture said about fragrance, I pondered as I looked for the chocolate bits. "*God, who . . . through us spreads the fragrance of the knowledge of Him everywhere*," flashed in my mind as I remembered Christ's words.

Fingering through index cards for my recipe, I questioned my life and the fragrance that arose. The flowers were an example that even one life could fill up vast regions.

While the children took turns mixing lumpy dough, I thought of others' lives and the airs that they gave . . . pessimism, optimism, confidence, and joy. Certainly I knew which conversations lifted and those which depressed. Laughter, challenge, and expectancy were the notes that brightened my day.

With a skirmish developing over licking the beaters, my frustration mounted. Minutes before pointing a finger and descending with gloom, I was reminded again of the lovely lilac. Carefully I chose my words as the fight went on. I would not let my words produce a torrent of tears and coat the children's festivity with a blanket of judgment.

Solving the problem of coated beaters was not so difficult with soft words and positive choices. Such a simple solution could also be used with other oppositions that flowed through life.

As I gazed at the vase with beautiful purple petals, I was freshly reminded of my witness in life. While my children washed their batter-licked beaters, I humbly offered a prayer:

"Thank You, Lord, for the message of lilacs. Remind me again of the far-reaching effects of my unkind words, gossip, anger, and discouragement. Help me to always see the value of practicing and sharing encouragement. Let me dwell on things that are good, fair, and pure.

"Assist me in filling my house with the fragrance of goodness. And when I leave my home, help me not to be a representative of evil, but to share Your joy. Father, thank You for springtime flowers, for Your love, and for the beautiful, heady fragrance that flows from both!"

Photograph © Nancy Matthews

Mother's Garden

Matthias Barr

A fresh little bud in my garden
with petals close-folded from view,
brightly nods me a cheery "Good morning,"
through the drops of a fresh bath of dew.

I must patiently wait its unfolding,
tho' I long its full beauty to see;
leave soft breezes and warm, tender sunshine
to perform the sweet office for me.

I may shield my fair baby blossom;
with trellis its weakness uphold;
with nourishment wisely sustain it,
and cherish its pure heart of gold.

Then, in good time, which is God's time,
developed by sunshine and shower,
some morning I'll find in the garden
where my bud was, a beautiful flower.

I LOVE LITTLE CHILDREN,
AND IT IS NOT A SLIGHT THING
WHEN THEY, WHO ARE FRESH
FROM GOD, LOVE US.
—CHARLES DICKENS

The Soul of a Child

Author Unknown

The soul of a child is the loveliest flower
that grows in the garden of God.
Its climb is from weakness to knowledge
    and power,
to the sky from the clay to the cloud.
To beauty and sweetness it grows under care.
Neglected, 'tis ragged and wild.
'Tis a plant that is tender, but wondrously rare:
the sweet, wistful soul of a child.

Be tender, O gardener, and give it its share
of moisture, of warmth and of light,
and let it not lack for the painstaking care
to protect it from frost and from blight.
A glad day will come when its bloom
    shall unfold;
it will seem that an angel has smiled,
reflecting a beauty and sweetness untold
in the sensitive soul of a child.

Photograph © Dennis Frates Photography

MOMMY PRAYING

Linda J. Burba

I could tell from the start that this day would be no exception. Three-year-old Matthew climbed into bed with me, lay there quietly for no more than two minutes, with his ice-cold feet robbing warmth from my legs, and then began squirming.

"Let's wake up, Mom. I want breakfast." I grunted assent, though my eyelids were still heavy with sleep, and my head burrowed into the pillow a bit deeper. When the whining picked up in intensity, I knew Matt would soon wake his twin brother, Michael, and baby Mark. I got out of bed.

So the morning started. After breakfast, I gave Mark his bath while Matt and Mike pulled all their toys into the living-room floor. Then they ransacked three drawers in their bedroom, fought over who got to wear the new yellow socks, and came out crying because, alas, this was a wash day and favorite clothes were still in the laundry. I pulled out some alternative shirts and pants and tried to convince the twins that these would do.

Soon Mark began rubbing his eyes and fussing a little. It was time for his morning nap. Another diaper change and he was down in his crib for the time being.

The twins by now were all dressed— underpants backwards on Matt, shirt backwards on Mike, but nevertheless dressed. We sat on the couch and read a children's story, knelt down to pray before the day's play, and they were off.

This would be one of the two quiet times of the day. I had learned early in my Christian life, long before we had children, that my spiritual well-being is dependent on daily communion with God. But finding a time of quiet was another question. With three small boys, there never seemed enough chance to concentrate on "effective, fervent prayer," eyes closed and shutting out the world. After putting a load of wash in the machine, making beds, and straightening the house a little, there was barely time for the reading part of my devotions. *I'll pray during their afternoon naps*, my mind noted.

I sat down with the Bible at the kitchen table where I could see the front yard. I'd been reading through the psalms, noticing what distinct mood changes David went through. I think David must have understood mothers.

Shortly, Matt ran inside. "Mom, Laura and Jennifer say I'm 'icky,'" he complained. "They hate boys." I told him to ignore them. He didn't know what "ignore" meant, but it seemed to satisfy him that he had tattled. He ran back out.

I read a few more verses.

Matt sauntered back. "I need a rag."

"What for?"

"To wash the porch!" (He used an isn't-it-obvious tone.)

Rather than argue, I got him a rag. I vaguely wondered where he would get the water but decided I would solve that problem if it arose. Right now I was trying to have my devotions.

Mike came to the window walking stiff-legged, as if he'd delayed a certain duty too long. That was not the problem, I soon found out. "Mom, Matt

Photograph © Joy Brown/Shutterstock

wetted me with the hose." I yelled at Matt to turn off that hose, and I got Mike some dry clothes.

I read a few more verses. The next interruption in my reading was Mike's too. "Can I go bare-feet?"

"Of course," I responded without enthusiasm. "Put your shoes in the house so the puppy won't carry them away."

"Can't I just put them on the picnic table?" Always an alternative plan!

"Sure." And I got through a few more verses.

Matt came around. "Mom, can I take off my shoes like Mike?"

"Okay. Put your shoes on the picnic table so Clipper won't carry them off."

"I thought we're s'posed to put our shoes in the house."

"Either place is all right today." I was trying to read.

Finally, they went off to play at their friend's house. Mark awakened as I finished the psalm I was reading. Its praise section was uplifting, and for a moment I reflected on the sentiments Paul expresses in another part of the Bible: "In whatsoever state I am, therewith to be content" (Philippians 4:11).

I hummed a tune as I resumed my tasks, remembering the day's beginning when I had knelt beside my bed for a few moments of prayer. I'd looked up and seen Matt's pleased smile as he knelt directly across from me, hands folded, listening. He had said, "I prayed to Jesus, too, Mom. And I thanked Him for my mommy praying here right now."

My moments with God's Word lift me. The prayers encourage me. And little lives are watching, listening, and learning from my daily example.

When the boys are grown up, they won't remember the interruptions. But I hope they will remember seeing Mom read her Bible and hearing her pray.

God Gave to Me a Child

James B. Singleton

God gave to me a child—and then I knew
the precious gift of life, the beating heart,
the little hand that clings in childish trust,
the shining eyes that are so much a part
of every moment in a parent's day;
a language that no words could ever say.

God gave to me a child—and then I knew
the joy of love fulfilled, the quiet peace
of home and fireside where, with strife denied,
the heart can calmly rest in love's release,
can gain strength in knowing angels stand
around little ones with guarding hand.

God gave to me a child—and then I knew
the parenthood of God, the eternal care
of He who keeps the night watch
    and never sleeps,
Who, when His children need Him,
    is always there.
I sought His kingdom for so long a while,
and then I found it in my little baby's smile.

SPRING *by Robert Duncan. Image © Robert Duncan*

Baby's Here...
Congratulations!

Mona K. Guldswog

Who would have thought
such tiny hands
so tightly furled
could hold my heart . . .
my brightest dreams . . .
my very world.

Only

Harriet Prescott Spofford

Something to live for came to the place,
something to die for maybe,
something to give even sorrow a grace,
and yet it was only a baby!

Cooing and laughter and gurgles and cries,
dimples for tenderest kisses,
chaos of hopes and of raptures and sighs,
chaos of fears and of blisses.

Last year, like all years, the rose and the thorn;
this year a wilderness maybe;
but heaven stooped under the roof on the morn
that it brought them only a baby!

Only a
Baby Small

Matthias Barr

Only a baby small
dropped from the skies;
only a laughing face,
two sunny eyes.

Only two cherry lips,
one chubby nose;
only two little hands,
ten little toes.

Only a golden head,
curly and soft;
only a tongue that wags
loudly and oft.

Only a little brain,
empty of thought;
only a little heart,
troubled with naught.

Only a tender flower,
sent us to rear;
only a life to love
while we are here.

Only a baby small,
never at rest;
small, but how dear to us,
God knoweth best.

At Baby's Bed

Betty W. Stoffel

Child of my heart, so fast asleep,
why do I tiptoe back to peep
through shadowed light at your little bed
and venture a hand to your pillowed head,
drawn by your features calm and sweet,
wrapped in your peace that is so complete?

Child of my heart, tucked in with care,
why do I stand so quietly there,
hushed in your every breath so deep,
loving you silently in your sleep,
warmed in a special wondrous way,
thinking what only the heart can say?

Child of my heart, it must be true
that God stands there and watches too,
for I feel as I study your little face
that reverence felt in a holy place.
Can it be that a mother's heart is led
to know God best at a baby's bed?

Sometime

Eugene Field

Last night, my darling, as you slept,
I thought I heard you sigh,
and to your little crib I crept,
and watched a space thereby.
Then bending down I kissed your brow,
for, oh, I love you so!
You are too young to know it now,
but sometime you shall know.

In a mother undefiled, prayer goeth on in sleep, as true and pauseless as the pulses do.
—ELIZABETH BARRETT BROWNING

THE LANGUAGE OF LULLABIES

Pamela Kennedy

The last time we visited our son and his family, I was finishing up the lunch dishes when I heard a voice coming from the baby's room. Listening in a bit more closely, I recognized a familiar tune, "Brahms' Lullaby," but the words weren't the ones I remembered. Later I asked my sweet daughter-in-law about what she was singing. "Oh it's a lullaby my Gramma used to sing. I don't remember the words, so I just make some up. Henry doesn't seem to mind."

I think she is on to something. Mothers have been singing their babies to sleep since ancient times, and if you listen to the words of some of those lullabies, it is clear the experience is much more about their sound than their meaning. The earliest lullaby lyrics on record are kept in the British Museum in London and are etched on a small clay tablet. They date from around 2000 BC in ancient Babylon (modern-day Iraq). We have

no idea about the melody, but the words are pretty scary, threatening the baby with dire consequences for crying and waking up the house gods.

A continent away, in Africa, a traditional lullaby warns a fussing baby to hush or risk being eaten by a hyena. Even the old favorite, "Rock-a-Bye Baby," first published in England in 1765, gives one pause. Sure, it starts out with a lovely sentiment about a baby being rocked by gentle breezes in the treetops, but before long, the branch breaks and both baby and cradle come crashing to the ground. In a more contemporary example illustrating the point that the language of lullabies isn't about the words, I recall a friend, who used to make up melodies for recipes from the *Southern Living Cookbook*. She maintained that, since her babies didn't understand what she was saying anyway, she might as well rock them to sleep while reading something of interest to her.

The language of lullabies, it would seem, has much more to do with sounds and rhythms than with the logic of the words. When singing to their babies, mothers often rock or sway while repeating phrases, rhymes, and soothing vowel sounds. While this action may seem intuitive to many, there is scientific research attesting to motion's effectiveness.

Dr. Colwyn Trevarthen, Emeritus Professor of Child Psychology and Psychobiology at the

University of Edinburgh, spent years documenting how rhythm and expressions of musicality in movement help parents give care and companionship to young children. Another researcher, Russian pediatrician Michael Lazarev, likens the mother's lullabies to an "acoustic bridge" between the baby's life in the womb and his or her life in the outside world, thus reinforcing the bonds between mother and child.

Scientific studies aside, most mothers just seem to know that singing to a fussy baby usually helps. It can be a classical lullaby like Brahms', a nursery rhyme like "Twinkle, Twinkle Little Star," a classic spiritual like "Swing Low, Sweet Chariot," that heartbreaker "Baby Mine" from the Disney movie, "Dumbo," or even an original song you make up on the spot. One of my children's favorites was a silly little ditty I made up as a takeoff on a popular '70s public service announcement that asked: Do you know where your children are? Here, with apologies to Rodgers and Hammerstein, are the lyrics:

Photograph © Nick Carter/GAP Interior Images Ltd.

Good night, Mr. Moon.
Good evening, Mrs. Star.
Are all your children home in bed?
Do you know where they are?

Are they dancing in the starlight?
Are they hiding in the dark?

Did they slide down a moonbeam
to play in the park?

Good night, Mr. Moon.
Good evening, Mrs. Star.
Are all your children home in bed?
Do you know where they are?

Those lyrics surely wouldn't win any contests, but they seemed to do the trick at bedtime as we snuggled in the old rocking chair watching the branches of the trees make moonlit shadows on the nursery wall. And perhaps that's the most important thing about the language of lullabies. It transcends rhythm and rhyme as well as research. It's the language of love between a mother and child, a language as old as time.

The Road to Slumber-Land

Mary D. Brine

What is the road to Slumber-Land,
and when does the baby go?
The road lies straight through Mother's
arms when the sun is sinking low.

He goes by the drowsy land of Nod
to the music of lullaby,
when all wee lambs are safe in the fold,
under the evening sky.

Two little tired, satiny feet,
from the shoe and stocking free;
two little palms together clasped
at the mother's patient knee.

Some baby words that are drowsily lisped
to the tender Shepherd's ear;
and a kiss that only a mother can place
on the brow of her baby dear.

A little round head which nestles at last
close to the mother's breast,
and then the lullaby, soft and low,
singing the song of rest.

And close and closer the blue-vein'd lids
are hiding the baby eyes,
as over the road to Slumber-Land
the dear little traveler hies.

For this is the way, through mother's arms,
all little babies go
to the beautiful city of Slumber-Land
when the sun is sinking low.

I Had a Mother Who Read to Me

Strickland Gillilan

I had a mother who read to me
sagas of pirates who scoured the sea,
cutlasses clenched in their yellow teeth,
"Blackbirds" stowed in the hold beneath.

I had a mother who read me lays
of ancient and gallant and golden days;
stories of Marmion and Ivanhoe,
which every boy has a right to know.

I had a mother who read me tales
of Gêlert the hound of the hills of Wales,
true to his trust till his tragic death,
faithfulness blent with his final breath.

I had a mother who read me the things
that wholesome life to the boy-heart brings—
stories that stir with an upward touch,
oh, that each mother of boys were such!

You may have tangible wealth untold;
caskets of jewels and coffers of gold.
Richer than I you can never be—
I had a mother who read to me.

A Song for My Mother—Her Stories

Anna Hempstead Branch

I always liked to go to bed—
it looked so dear and white.
Besides, my mother used to tell
a story every night.

The room was full of slumber lights,
of seas and ships and wings,
of Holy Grails and swords and knights
and beautiful, kind things.

And so she wove and wove and wove
her singing thoughts through mine.
I heard them murmuring through my sleep,
sweet, audible, and fine.

Beneath my pillow all night long
I heard her stories sing,
so spun through the enchanted sheet
was their soft shadowing.

Dear custom, stronger than the years—
then let me not grow dull!
Still every night my bed appears
friendly and beautiful!

Even now when I lie down to sleep,
it comes like a caress;
and still, somehow, my childish heart
expects a pleasantness.

I find in the remembering sheets
old stories told by her,
and they are sweet as rosemary
and dim as lavender.

A MOM FOR ALL SEASONS

Kate Kellogg

When Father died, leaving Mother with four young children, she quickly adjusted to the dual role of mother and father. She learned to wield a hammer for necessary repairs, how to whitewash the garden fences as well as the dark, gloomy basement where the winter coal was stored, and how to turn her not particularly nimble fingers to making our clothes.

But what we children remember best was the frugal way she managed to keep us happy and amused all through the year. She taught us to skate and how to use that little turn-key to adjust the roller skates to our various-sized feet. Her firm arms held us upright on our first wobbly tries at bike riding.

The single bike used by the four of us (one size fits all) and the passed-around skates were extravagances. For very little she managed other pleasures. In summer we gathered the windfall apples from a friendly neighbor's garden and helped Mom to make apple butter, taking turns stirring the hissing, spitting mass. We watched as she ladled it into jars and helped her to store them in the cool darkness of the basement to later be enjoyed at winter breakfasts. As we poured it liberally onto our toast on winter mornings, Mom would always say, "It's better for you than butter," and we would chorus, "And cheaper."

In autumn she explained the neighborhood rules for "Kick the Can," and in winter she produced a bag of marbles. I can still remember my prize agate, fondly called an "aggie." A box of chalk was offered for drawing hopscotch patterns on the sidewalk.

However, when the windy days of March arrived, we were left gazing enviously at our friends flying their colored kites to glorious heights. How lovely the kites were dipping and jerking in the changing winds. We begged for our own. "No," said Mother firmly, "we can't afford kites for the four of you. We will make our own."

Eagerly we gathered round the table, confident that our resourceful Mother would fashion a kite that would be the envy of our friends. She took thin sticks of balsa wood and fashioned them into a cross, fastening the crossbar with a tack. Tissue paper from past gifts was sought, and she made a paste of flour and water to fasten the thin paper to the waiting frame. We knew something was missing. My older brother said, "Mom, a kite needs a tail."

"Of course," agreed our mother, as if she knew this all along. She went to her sewing basket, took out scraps of fabric, and instructed us to tear the material into thin strips. One by one pieces of long-gone dresses and discarded shirts were tied together into a long queue. We could recognize a patch of orange from the dress worn in first grade and brother's Sunday-best blue shirt, outgrown by all the younger siblings. It was a chain of our past lives.

AMISH QUILTSCAPE *by Rebecca Barker. Image © Rebecca Barker*

We weren't sure how long to make the tail, but about four feet seemed right. How to fasten this to the wooden frame? We never did manage to tie it exactly in the center for a balanced kite, but we were confident. When we woke the next morning, we were pleased to see a strong wind blowing. Out we went to "Windy Hill" and ran along the ground waiting for the kite to rise. Each took a turn, certain that he or she could sent it aloft after the other's failure. Finally we had to admit that while Mother had many talents, kite making was not one of them.

Mother smiled at our sad faces and said, "We'll compromise and buy one store kite, and you can take turns flying it." We eagerly marched off to the store and purchased a beauty of orange and red. How carefully we watched one another's performance until it was our turn, for there was always the danger of breaking or losing the delicate kite.

By the time, several weeks later, when one of us did snag it in the branches of a tall tree, we didn't mind too much, for baseball season had arrived and Mom was busy pitching her version of a "curve ball" to us. Our spring season had begun. The scarred bats and pummeled gloves didn't keep my brothers from doing well in Little League.

So from season to season, Mom devised inexpensive ways to keep us busy and happy, but best of all, she taught us the joy of sharing.

Side by Side

Sherri Waas Shunfenthal

Side by side
with my daughter,
making a cake from
scratch:

flour,
butter,
water,
eggs,

sugar to add sweetness
to our day.
We stir and stir.

Memories:
myself as a little girl,
baking joyfully with
my mother,
side by side.

Kitchen Memories

Marilyn Driscoll

From my kitchen comes good cooking—
fine foods, made by mixing and baking,
guided by my cookbooks, but more
by the instinct born in me
and nourished in my mother's kitchen.
Although I learned there, I remember
no formal training; instead I remember
just being there,
watching, doing, imitating,
while good-food aromas filled the room
and hungry people came and went.

I sat on a high green stool
that twirled as my little girl's feet
reached for rungs just the right height
for starting or stopping the turning stool.

"Taste this," my mother would say.
"Do you want to lick the beater?"
"You can scrape the pan."

And I'd spoon off
sweet, toasted crumbs. Delicious.
      Nothing wasted.
Nothing has tasted better since.
There were no fancy foods,
      but thrifty meals—
chuck roast in an iron pot,
      chicken fricassee with rice,
or thick split-pea soup with
      bones to be retrieved
from the deep kettle.

From my kitchen come
      more exotic foods
than pot roast and pea soup,
but nothing that tastes better
comes from my kitchen
than what I learned to cook
atop the twirling green stool.

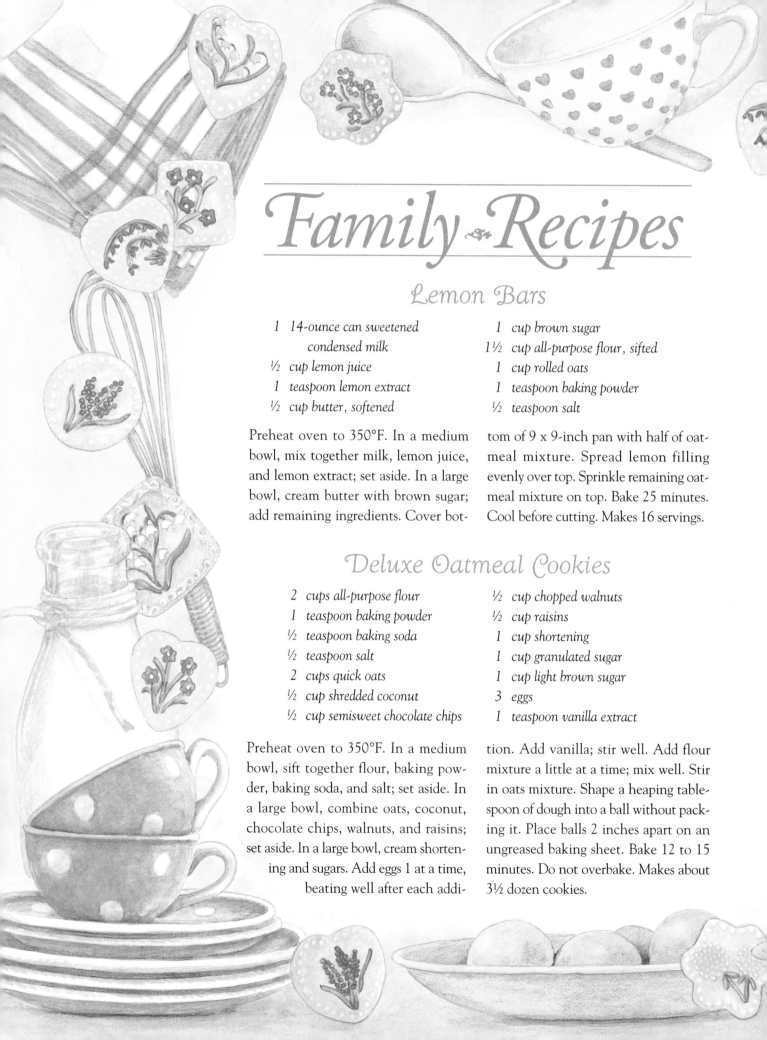

Family · Recipes

Lemon Bars

1	14-ounce can sweetened condensed milk
½	cup lemon juice
1	teaspoon lemon extract
½	cup butter, softened
1	cup brown sugar
1½	cup all-purpose flour, sifted
1	cup rolled oats
1	teaspoon baking powder
½	teaspoon salt

Preheat oven to 350°F. In a medium bowl, mix together milk, lemon juice, and lemon extract; set aside. In a large bowl, cream butter with brown sugar; add remaining ingredients. Cover bottom of 9 x 9-inch pan with half of oatmeal mixture. Spread lemon filling evenly over top. Sprinkle remaining oatmeal mixture on top. Bake 25 minutes. Cool before cutting. Makes 16 servings.

Deluxe Oatmeal Cookies

2	cups all-purpose flour
1	teaspoon baking powder
½	teaspoon baking soda
½	teaspoon salt
2	cups quick oats
½	cup shredded coconut
½	cup semisweet chocolate chips
½	cup chopped walnuts
½	cup raisins
1	cup shortening
1	cup granulated sugar
1	cup light brown sugar
3	eggs
1	teaspoon vanilla extract

Preheat oven to 350°F. In a medium bowl, sift together flour, baking powder, baking soda, and salt; set aside. In a large bowl, combine oats, coconut, chocolate chips, walnuts, and raisins; set aside. In a large bowl, cream shortening and sugars. Add eggs 1 at a time, beating well after each addition. Add vanilla; stir well. Add flour mixture a little at a time; mix well. Stir in oats mixture. Shape a heaping tablespoon of dough into a ball without packing it. Place balls 2 inches apart on an ungreased baking sheet. Bake 12 to 15 minutes. Do not overbake. Makes about 3½ dozen cookies.

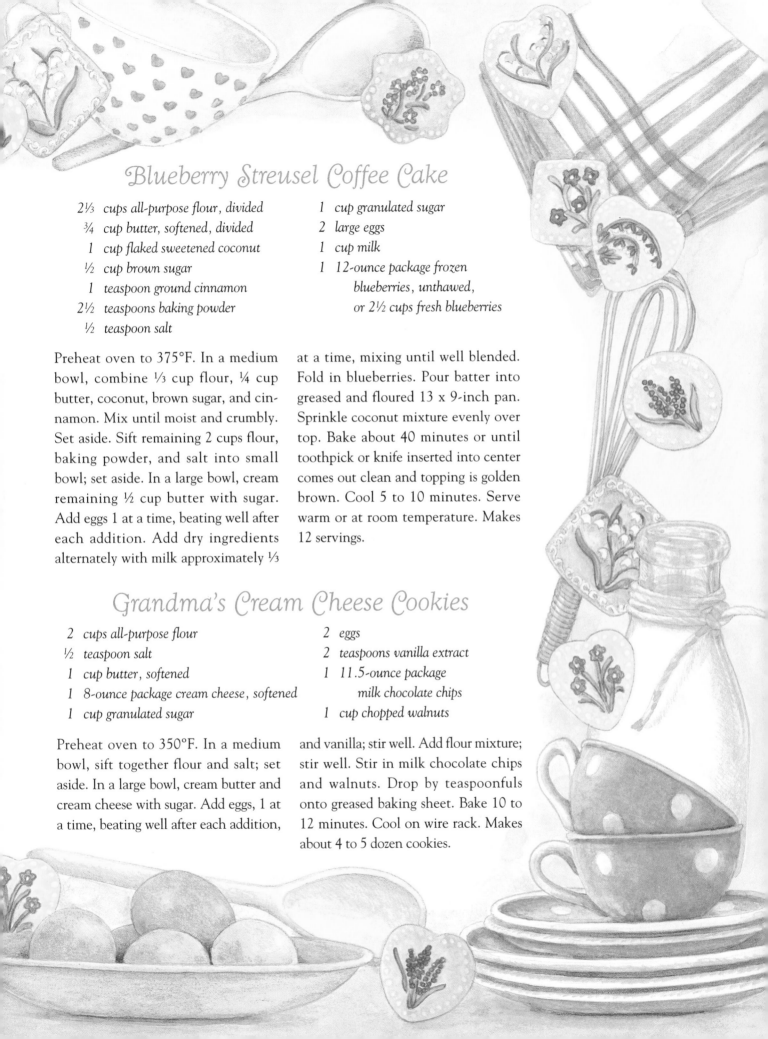

Blueberry Streusel Coffee Cake

2⅓ cups all-purpose flour, divided	1 cup granulated sugar
¾ cup butter, softened, divided	2 large eggs
1 cup flaked sweetened coconut	1 cup milk
½ cup brown sugar	1 12-ounce package frozen
1 teaspoon ground cinnamon	blueberries, unthawed,
2½ teaspoons baking powder	or 2½ cups fresh blueberries
½ teaspoon salt	

Preheat oven to 375°F. In a medium bowl, combine ⅓ cup flour, ¼ cup butter, coconut, brown sugar, and cinnamon. Mix until moist and crumbly. Set aside. Sift remaining 2 cups flour, baking powder, and salt into small bowl; set aside. In a large bowl, cream remaining ½ cup butter with sugar. Add eggs 1 at a time, beating well after each addition. Add dry ingredients alternately with milk approximately ⅓ at a time, mixing until well blended. Fold in blueberries. Pour batter into greased and floured 13 x 9-inch pan. Sprinkle coconut mixture evenly over top. Bake about 40 minutes or until toothpick or knife inserted into center comes out clean and topping is golden brown. Cool 5 to 10 minutes. Serve warm or at room temperature. Makes 12 servings.

Grandma's Cream Cheese Cookies

2 cups all-purpose flour	2 eggs
½ teaspoon salt	2 teaspoons vanilla extract
1 cup butter, softened	1 11.5-ounce package
1 8-ounce package cream cheese, softened	milk chocolate chips
1 cup granulated sugar	1 cup chopped walnuts

Preheat oven to 350°F. In a medium bowl, sift together flour and salt; set aside. In a large bowl, cream butter and cream cheese with sugar. Add eggs, 1 at a time, beating well after each addition, and vanilla; stir well. Add flour mixture; stir well. Stir in milk chocolate chips and walnuts. Drop by teaspoonfuls onto greased baking sheet. Bake 10 to 12 minutes. Cool on wire rack. Makes about 4 to 5 dozen cookies.

A TOAST TO MOTHERS

Patricia Penton Leimbach

Long before my mother's face came sharply into focus in my mind, I could have described her hands. They were small for one who seemed so large—the skin stretched tautly over her knuckles. Over the backs of them, where the blue veins swelled and relaxed with the motion of her fingers, the skin was shiny and covered with masses of freckles.

My mother's hands were more at my eye level than was her face, but surely my awareness of them bespoke the loving care they extended. I remember those hands washing my smaller ones at the kitchen sink. I remember her hands cradling me in an armchair as she read to my brothers and me. And I recall her touch on my warm forehead as I lay ill on the couch.

I remember her hands mashing my potatoes, pouring the tea, and working at the washboard and the wringer and the clothesline. I remember those hands, all flour and dough, as she kneaded the bread, scattered feed for the chickens, and pulled sweet corn in the field. My mother's hands gave me the secure feeling that the world existed for me and that I would never want for anything.

No mother need ever belabor the point that she works hard for her family. A small child defines his mother in terms of the many things she does for him. One little girl in my son's class, groping for the scope of her mother's ministrations says, "She does so much I can't even say them all."

As I grew older my focus on my mother shifted from her hands to her face. I knew by then that it was a big world, that I did not have this woman all to myself. But it didn't seem to matter. Her response to each of us was wholehearted—one child, one mother. It is in this acknowledgment of a child's "gifts" of gratitude, a handful of short-stemmed flowers, a clumsy attempt to make a bed, or a wrinkled arithmetic paper with a star, that a child finds or fails to find the longed-for acceptance.

It was a well-guarded secret between my mother and me that I was princess of the earth. When I discovered—very soon—that everyone didn't share that view, I did the best I could to conceal the fact from Mother. I could bear the truth that I was just another girl among girls, but I wasn't sure that she could. The truth was, of course, that my mother had two princesses and five princes. No one has ever convinced her that they were otherwise.

Love certainly works her greatest miracle through good mothers—their serving hands, their gentle approving faces, their unswerving faith in their children. There is no gift a mother gives a child more important than believing in him so strongly that eventually he comes to believe in himself.

Some Small Delight
Milly Walton

Give me this day some small delight,
some simple joy to cheer my soul,
a singing bird upon the bough,
a drifting cloud in sky's blue bowl;
the pealing laughter of my child,
the glint of sunlight on his hair,
the feel of his warm hand in mine,
of these dear things make me aware;

a blossom in the garden spot,
the music of the poplar trees,
the fragrance of a dew-washed earth,
what could enchant me more than these?
Grant me the perception that I may
live deeply through this chartless day,
and when I go to sleep tonight
be thankful for each small delight.

Thoughts of a Busy Mother
Katherine Cahill

If I can't find the time to wash the floor,
who will remember or care?
If I don't patch the hole in their
    old blue jeans,
they can wear another pair.

The dust can sit right where it is,
for tomorrow there will be more.
If the day is too short to bake a cake,
I can always run to the store.

But if I forget to wipe a tear
or kiss an injured knee,
to cheer a frown, turn it upside down
till they're chuckling with glee:

if I would fail to stop and chat
when their tales are filled with woe,
to listen for unspoken words
that only sad eyes show,

if I missed a chance to see the world
through their precious eyes . . .
a dandelion, a crawly bug,
a rainbow in the sky,

then I've missed a chance to
    share the day
with one I hold most dear;
for God was knocking at my heart,
and I was too busy to hear.

A Time of Joy

Elizabeth Symon

The buttercups and dandelions
and daisies—well-known names—
we gathered in the garden then
for my young daughter's games.

"Let's see, do you like butter?"
she would ask me with a grin
as she held glossy petals up
to glow beneath my chin.
"You do, Mommy, you do, just look!
You do!" she'd cry with glee.
The gold reflection of the flower
was there, we would agree.

And with a wealth of little flowers,
she'd make a daisy chain
by threading all the tiny stems
in, out, and in again.
When this ploy tired, she then would take
one daisy from the lot,
and picking petals one by one,
play "Loves Me, Loves Me Not!"

And if the dandelions had bloomed
and they were past their prime,
she'd joy in blowing their seed "clocks"
to help her tell the time.
"A one, a two, a four," she'd puff.
"I think I missed out three,
or should that one be five o'clock?
Can you help count with me?"

Oh, springtimes past and long ago,
a time of fun and flowers—
I wish I could call back again
those happy, carefree hours!

LETTER TO A SON ON MOTHER'S DAY

Patricia Penton Leimbach

Once I lay in labor clutching friendly hands and breathing deeply and yearning for an end; and when the fog lifted they lay a small form in my arms, and it was Mother's Day. A hundred nights I sat upright and asked, "Is he breathing?" and ran to a cradle and touched your warm body, and it was Mother's Day.

On sunny afternoons you stood in your crib and reached for a sunbeam—Mother's Day. You grasped for tangible things, baubles I cherished that broke at your touch, and I wept and knew Mother's Day.

I have heard your screams and run with a towel to stop your flowing blood and sat in emergency rooms stroking your head and holding your hot hand and praying on Mother's Day.

I have looked at group pictures of disheveled children and seen only one face—yours. I have sat in auditoriums where out of a hundred performing children, only you stood out.

I have watched you at play with strange children when you stood aside, shy and frightened; and I have watched you lead a charge on the haymow, with all the neighborhood in pursuit. I have seen you unite with them in frantic projects and then gone at a tug of your hand to inspect tree houses, tent houses, caves, leaf piles, snow forts, and snowmen—always it was Mother's Day.

I have scolded and chastised and paddled; cajoled, laughed, applauded, advised. I have untangled fish lines, tied tails for kites, sewed marble bags, laced ice skates. I have made milk shakes, baked cookies, packed picnics, performed the many joys for you that complicate and enrich a mother's day.

I have screamed at you in my impatience over unimportant things and gone to you in your hurt and apologized. I have recoiled at words or deeds "good" children do not tender toward their mothers and been overwhelmed with forgiveness when you came to say, "I'm sorry." It was a mother's day.

I have shared you with your father and delighted in the sharing. There were times of arbitration when I explained you to each other, and times when you drew apart for father's days I could not share.

I have given you over to other mentors—to teachers, ministers, 4-H leaders, coaches—and been grateful to them for what they gave you of themselves, proud to share my mother's days. But I have been jealous that always you gave them your best face, while at home you bared them all, which is as it should be.

You have come clattering into the house with the smell of schoolrooms heavy upon you and shouted, "Mama! Guess what?" And I have guessed a thousand times and known that the only truth was you wanted me there—Mother's Day.

From the window I have watched you at play and at work, developing strength and independence, and I have felt the tug of the "silver cord." The world claims you more and more, and I go to bed not always knowing where you are, but trusting you and loving you always.

Photograph © Pernilla Bergdahl/GAP Photos Ltd.

You bring me a plant for Mother's Day or a handmade card, a paperweight or pincushion; or you bring me nothing more than you have already given, and certainly you need not. I gave you life, and every fulfilling day since, you have given me back something wonderful of yourself on a succession of endless Mother's Days.

Young Mother

Elinor Lennen

But yesterday she was a child;
an infant, scarcely days before.
How can this change be reconciled?
Swiftly, as through a secret door,
come ancient wisdom, utmost grace,
and womanhood as her bequest.
She holds the promise of our race
like a medallion at her breast.

New Vision

Jean Hogan Dudley

My little girl and I go hand in hand
beside the summer fields still fresh with grass
and question all the things of sky and land,
each stone and tree, each blossom that we pass.

She asks, "Why are the rosebuds curled so tight?
What holds the golden sun above the world?
Who shoots the arrowed birds upon their flight?
How long have purple hillsides been unfurled?"

And I, who learned the truths that wise men tell,
for all of nature in the earth and sky,
and who have known these beauties long and well,
until with dullest gaze, I passed them by,
now see through childhood's bright, unclouded view,
and find all things miraculous and new!

FIELD NOTES ON AN EMPTY NEST

Cindy La Ferle

Working in our perennial garden last week, I found an empty bird's nest on the brick walk leading to the backyard. I'm guessing the nest fell from a nearby silver maple, or maybe a neighbor found it while jogging and left it by the gate for us to admire.

Not much larger than a cereal bowl, the nest now perches indoors on a shelf near my writing desk. Crafted from hundreds of delicate twigs, strands of grass, and dried moss, it's truly a work of art—and a timely reminder to prepare for my son's return to college after the long summer break. I've been discussing this tender rite of passage with other middle-aged mothers, all of whom agree that there has to be a better term to describe our next season of parenting—a phrase that doesn't sound as final or forlorn as "the empty nest."

Our nests, after all, are not completely empty. Not yet. My only child, for example, still has a bedroom at home in addition to a loft in a crowded dormitory on the other side of the state.

But a lot has changed since my son started college. For starters, the calendar in our kitchen now shows some blank spaces and is no longer decorated with colorful sticky notes to remind us of band concerts, school conferences, football games, and carpool schedules.

At first, this was not cause for celebration. I'd suddenly become what our high school moth-ers' club affectionately refers to as one of the "alumni moms." I mourned the inevitable loss of my role as a hands-on parent. And despite the fact that I was left with a cleaner, quieter house, I missed all the athletic shoes and flip-flops piled near the back door. I missed the hungry teenagers snacking at my kitchen counter after school. I missed bumping into other parents at our weekly school functions—and I wondered if life would ever be the same.

Life isn't the same, but I'm okay with that now. I've come to realize that a mom is always a mom, though her parenting role evolves and changes over time.

Not long ago, I stayed at my own mother's place for a few weeks while I recovered from major surgery. When I apologized for disrupting Mom's normal routine, she said, "My home will always be your home too." Of course, I found comfort in that. Yet at the same time, I realized how grateful I was that my parents had encouraged me, years ago, to spread my wings and create a loving home and family of my own.

It's hard to believe my son starts another year of college this month. I'm still not very good at saying good-bye when his dad and I leave him at the dormitory and steer back to the expressway. I usually manage to compose myself until I notice the tearful parents of col-lege freshmen going through this bittersweet

THE PEEPING TOMS—KIDS *by Lee Kromschroeder. Artwork provided courtesy of the artist and Wild Wings (800-445-4833, www.wildwings.com)*

ritual for the first time. But it does get easier with each new school term.

So, is my nest half full or half empty?

Reflecting on the small bird's nest perched near my desk, I'm at peace with the idea that our household is just one stop on our son's path to his future. He'll be flying back and forth over the next couple of years or so. And hopefully, patience and love will be the threads that weave our family together, no matter how far he travels.

To "His Mother"

Author Unknown

"Mother-in-law," they say, and yet,
somehow I simply can't forget
'twas you who watched his baby ways,
who taught him his first hymn of praise,

who smiled on him with loving pride
when he first toddled by your side;
and as I think of this today,
methinks I would much rather say
    just "Mother."

"Mother-in-law," but oh, 'twas you
who taught him to be kind and true;
when he was tired, almost asleep,
'twas to your arms he used to creep;

and when he'd bruised his tiny knee,
'twas you who kissed it tenderly;
when he was sad you cheered him, too,
and so I'd rather speak of you as "Mother."

"Mother-in-law," they say, and yet
somehow I never shall forget
how very much to you I owe
because you taught him how to grow;

you trained your son to look above;
you made of him the man I love,
and so I think of that today—
Ah! with thankful heart I'll say,
    "our Mother."

To My Other Mother

Judy Nilson

You are the mother I received
the day I wed your son,
and I just want to thank you, Mom,
for loving things you've done.

You've given me a gracious man
with whom I share my life.
You are his lovely mother,
and I, his lucky wife.

You used to pat his little head,
and now I hold his hand.
You raised in love a little boy
and then gave me the man.

Knitting

Barbara Crooker

My grandmother's needles
force the soft gray yarn
into patterns as old as Europe.
She came from a family of tailors
and gave each grandchild an afghan
of her own design.
The colors glow like January fire;
the stitches are perfect,
cabled with love.

My mother also knits
from patterns and pictures:
mittens with snowflakes
and Fair Isle socks.
Does she weave in June days
of yellow light, the babies
quietly piling blocks, the clean smell
of steam from dampened laundry?

My older daugther tries to knit, too,
but her hands can't master the needles,
so she pretends and spends hours
in a tangle of wool and steel.
She is already a maker
of emperor's cloth.
See the fine patterns?
    the royal colors?
    the designs more beautiful than stars?

And here I sit, like a bear in February,
huddled in yards of wool, skeined up in love,
clicking my pen across the page.
I take words and knit them back in poems.
Something could be made of this.

To an Unborn Grandchild

Isla Paschal Richardson

Across the waiting hours I send my love
to welcome you. We should have much in common,
you and I, holding so dear the one whose life links ours.
Let us be friends.

This world to which you come is vastly interesting,
and gloriously worthwhile its span of life.
Think clearly, and look up. Life can be fine and strong.
I shall not lecture nor admonish, nor prod you
    with ambition.
One thing, just this one thing I ask of you:
help me to pay a debt. You are the only one who can.
(Ah, it will be years and years—and even then
you may not ever know the depth of love
    she holds for you,
the one whom you call Mother!)

Do this for me:
from that first heaven-born moment
when she looks into your dewy,
    wondering eyes,
and dimpled, rose-leaf fingers cling to hers,
please bring into her life
as much joy and sunshine
as she has given mine.

Through My Window

GRANNY RULES

Pamela Kennedy

I was a late bloomer. My children didn't come along until I was in my thirties, and then they didn't get married until they were near their thirties; now that I'm collecting Social Security, I finally have my first grandchild, born just over a year ago. What this all adds up to is that for decades I have been something of an outsider as my peers discussed grandparenting. Although I had nothing to share, I decided to profit from their experiences and thus compiled my observations into what I call "Granny Rules."

Rule #1: You don't have to be called "Grandma" if you don't want to be. I personally know a Tu-tu, a Nona, a Nana, a Gammie, a Maw-maw, and a Gramma D.

Rule #2: Don't start any traditions you don't want to continue . . . forever! I know a woman who thought it would be tons of fun to have a two-week "Granny Camp" one summer with her long-distance grandchildren. Now she spends fifty weeks every year prepping for this annual event that features a different theme each summer. Last year was "Space" and included time at the planetarium, making telescopes, creating astronaut costumes, and building an eight-foot rocket ship with an old refrigerator carton. She told me she's already researching "Knights and Maidens" for next year and wondering how to fashion a suit of armor. Yikes!

Rule #3: Don't speak your mind unless you're willing to live with the consequences. My friend Linda says honesty is usually the best policy, but not so much when you're a grandma. To illustrate she shared about a time when she and her husband traveled to watch their three grandchildren for ten days while their parents were out of town. Let's just say that Linda's style of parenting and her daughter-in-law's weren't quite in sync. After returning home, Linda sent a letter to her son and daughter-in-law saying, among other things (and this is a direct quote), "You had better make some changes over there! I'm telling you, the inmates are running the asylum!" She didn't hear from her son for about six months, and it has taken years to mend those fences! Her advice: "Unless they are killing one another, don't say anything!"

Rule #4: Realize that you don't have to live up to the examples set by any other grandmas. My friend Shelley is a gifted stitchery artist. She draws her own patterns on quilt blocks and then fills them in with tiny embroidery and counted cross-stitch, creating beautiful colored pictures which she crafts into magnificent personalized quilts for her grandchildren. My college roommate, Annie, plants gardens and discusses botany with her granddaughter, and my friend Vicki taught her grandson to surf last summer. Jenna attends all her grandchildren's sporting events, and Laura and her grandson run 5Ks together. I get a migraine just imagining counted cross-stitch, and my legs cramp up watching a 5K. I'm thinking a trip to the library might be fun, especially if we catch a ladybug on the way.

Rule #5: You are not the expert. There are about a gazillion of those online and in print, and parents can find someone to support or debunk just about any child-rearing theory that has ever existed. Whether you think a baby should be lugged around and nursed until he's six years old or put on a schedule at six weeks, no one cares! Just smile and nod and be thankful you get to hold the baby at least some of the time.

Rule #6: Never say, "I told you so!" When your children acknowledge some truth about childrearing that you mentioned months ago, let them think it was their own idea. Smile graciously and be quiet, allowing them to believe they are brilliant.

Photograph © Gayvoronskaya Yana/Shutterstock

Rule #7: (This is the most important rule of all.) Enjoy every scrap of time you have with your grandchildren. Drink in the sweet fragrance of their freshly washed hair. Nuzzle the softness of their little necks. Marvel at the perfect symmetry of their tiny toes. And realize that they are God's way of rewarding you for all the years you spent raising their parents!

Time of Love
Amy Cassidy

Life was filled with special times
when my child was young and small,
times of love and happiness . . .
my heart has kept them all!

Now life is bringing back those times
in a new and lovely way,
times of love and happiness . . .
I'm a grandmother today!

A Lovely Surprise
Kay Andrew

Life has started all over for me;
the young years of happiness
have come again in a sweeter form
than a mother could ever guess.
The love and devotion I gave my child
I thought I could give no other,
but life held a lovely surprise for me—
this year I became a grandmother.

Small Girl Growing
Gladys Mckee

She is a giggle
surrounded by curl,
busily growing
into a girl.
She is a wiggle,
all hug and kiss,
making you do
what you would rather miss.

She thinks doors and drawers
should be opened wide;
I tie them, I tape them,
but she gets inside.
I think I'll survive her;
I spoil and I pet her
and let her do things
that her mother won't let her.

Mothers
Lela Bernard

With gentle hands God
made the flowers,
fashioning them with care.
He brushed the sky with
pink and gold,
leaving a sunset there;
beautified the earth with trees—
these works and countless others;
but for His greatest masterpiece,
God created mothers.

ISBN-13: 978-0-8249-1345-8

Published by Ideals Publications
A Guideposts Company
Nashville, Tennessee
www.idealsbooks.com

Printed and bound in the U.S.A.
Printed on Weyerhaeuser Lynx. The paper used in this publication meets the minimum requirements of American National Standard for Information Sciences—Permanence of Paper for Printed Library Materials, ANSI Z39.48-1984.

Publisher, Peggy Schaefer
Editor, Melinda L. R. Rumbaugh
Copy Editors, Robin Crouch and Debra Wright
Designer, Marisa Jackson
Permissions Editor, Kristi West

Cover: Photograph © Nancy Matthews
Inside front cover: *Grandmother's Flower Garden* by Rebecca Barker. Image © Rebecca Barker
Inside back cover: *Fireflies* by Rebecca Barker. Image © Rebecca Barker
Additional art credits: Art on pages 1, 12–13, 30, 40–41, and back cover by Kathy Rusynyk; background texture page 6, image © pashabo/iStockphoto; the following pages contain art © [the artist]/Shutterstock.com: 6, Denis Barbulat; 11, Astromonkey; 16, joyart; 28, andere andrea petrlik; 36–37, 501room; 42, Chekmareva Irina; 44, Moljavka; 48, Kiril Stanchev; 48–49, kiya-nochka; 50, Angie Makes; 54, Zhanna Smolyar and A-R-T; 56–57, Renata Novackova; 58, Denis Barbulat; 63, Moljavka.

Look for Ideals magazine on Facebook: www.Facebook.com/IdealsMagazine
Readers are invited to submit original poetry and prose for possible use in future publications. Please send no more than four typed submissions to: Magazine Submissions, Ideals Publications, 2630 Elm Hill Pike, Suite 100, Nashville, Tennessee 37214. Manuscripts will be returned if a self-addressed stamped envelope is included.

ACKNOWLEDGMENTS:

BURBA, LINDA J. "Mommy Praying" from *Guideposts Magazine*, copyright © September 1977 by Guideposts. All rights reserved. Used by permission. RICHARDSON, ISLA PASCHAL. "To an Unborn Grandchild" from *My Heart Waketh*, copyright © 1947 by Branden Publishing. All rights reserved. Used by permission.

OUR THANKS to the following authors or their heirs: Lela Bernard, Bea Bourgeois, Katherine Cahill, Barbara Crooker, Grace Noll Crowell, Marilyn Driscoll, Jean Hogan Dudley, Marie B. Fouts, Strickland Gillilan, Mona K. Guldswog, Kate Kellogg, Pamela Kennedy, Cynthia G. LaFerle, Irene Larsen, Elinor Lennen, Patricia Penton Leimbach, Judy Nilson, Sherri Waas Shunfenthal, Diane Skinner, James B. Singleton, Betty W. Stoffel, Elizabeth Symon, Milly Walton, and Elisabeth Weaver Winstead. Scripture quotations, unless otherwise indicated, are taken from King James Version (KJV). Scripture quotation marked RSV is from the Revised Standard Version of the Bible, copyright © 1946, 1952, and 1971 the Division of Christian Education of the National Council of the Churches of Christ in the United States of America. Used by permission. All rights reserved.

Every effort has been made to establish ownership and use of each selection in this book. If contacted, the publisher will be pleased to rectify any inadvertent errors or omissions in subsequent editions.